TABLE OF CONTENTS

1

GENERAL INSTRUCTIONS

MAKING A STENCIL

A couple of the projects in this book require you to make a stencil. We'll use Contact Brand clear shelf paper for this. You could try other brands of sticky-backed paper but I've used a couple of different ones that haven't worked too well, so I prefer the Contact brand.

You'll need to trace the object of your stencil onto your surface first. Then cut a piece of the adhesive paper about 2" wider than the design all the way around. Remove the backing paper from the shelf paper and place the sticky paper into position, centering it over the design. Gently press down around the edges of the design to ensure a good, flat adhesion. Cut along the design lines with an X-Acto knife and remove the interior, cut-out section. Again, press down along the edges of the cut out design to ensure a tight fit. Apply the paint as per the instructions, and then gently remove the stencil. Never dry the paint with a hairdryer before removing the stencil or you'll leave excess adhesive on your painted surface.

Gently rub your fingers around the outside of the painted design. If the area feels tacky at all, remove the adhesive with Goo Gone. Once the entire adhesive has been removed, dry the paint with a hair dryer.

USING LETTER STENCILS

A few of these projects use letter stencils. Each letter needs to be stenciled individually. To begin, draw a faint horizontal line in pencil or chalk as a guide for placement. For words that are centered, find the center letter and start your stenciling with that letter. For words that have a painted object to the left of the word, line up the first letter of the word and start stenciling there. For words that have a painted object to the right of the word, position the last letter, or punctuation mark, first and start stenciling there. Keep in mind that some letters are wider than others so

that affects the amount of space the word consumes. You also need to "eye-ball" the spacing between your letters. Some letters look better closer together than others so don't plan on having equal space between each letter.

Having said all that, it's best to practice stenciling the word on a piece of tracing paper. Then you can place the tracing paper on the painted surface and check for positioning and spacing.

To apply the paint, dip a Round Scumbler brush into a puddle of paint, wipe off most of the paint from the brush onto a paper towel, and then gently stipple the color into the stencil holes. You can make this as textured or as solid as you like.

USING FAUX GLAZE MEDIUM/ MOPPING

All floats and background glazing are done with Faux Glazing medium. The medium slows down the working time of the paint. That means, you can apply color for a float then use a mop to gently pounce the edge that's supposed to be soft and faded. For background glazing, apply the medium, brush on paint, not too thinly, and then pounce with the duster/stippler to soften and blend the color. Wipe the mop brushes regularly to remove excess paint. For smaller areas, use the Maxine's mop.

To keep the mops clean, dampen the center of a paper towel with a little water. Swish the dirty brush in the water spot then wipe the brush on a dry, clean spot on the towel. Repeat until brush comes clean. You could also use baby wipes to clean the brush.

Always make sure you dry the paint/medium well before proceeding with the next step…you might lift the color otherwise. Use a hair dryer to help speed drying time. Just make sure you let the piece cool before applying more medium or paint. The heat could cause the medium or paint to dry too quickly.

USING TAPE

I ALWAYS use low tack painters' tape. Too much paint has been lifted off in my life for me to want to use any other product. However, this tape also has serious leakage problems. So I solve that by stippling or sponging on color when I've taped off the surface. If I don't have water anywhere near the paint or tape and if I don't have too much paint on my sponge or brush, then the chances of paint leaking under the tape are greatly reduced.

SCUMBLING

Scumbling is the process of applying thin layers of color to the surface. Scumbling creates soft edges. To scumble, load the dry scumbler brush with paint then wipe the brush on a paper towel, removing most of the paint. Hold the brush about half way up the handle; place the bristles at a 45 degree angle on the surface then gently move the brush in a tight, circular motion to deposit color. Do not press hard on the brush. A nice, soft touch gives you a nice, soft layer of color. Reload as needed. To clean the brush, see "Using Faux Glazing Medium" above.

DRYBRUSHING

This is similar to scumbling —you load the dry brush and wipe off the excess paint — but, here, you slap the brush on the surface to create chunky layers of color. This color application is not soft, and it is not subtle.

CRACKLE MEDIUMS

Two different types of crackle medium are used on some of these projects – the regular Crackle Medium and the Fine Finish crackle. The regular crackle is a sandwich crackle. This means you need to base coat the area; apply the crackle medium; let the medium dry then top coat with a contrasting color of paint. The thicker you apply the medium and the top coat, the thicker the cracks will be. The Fine Finish Crackle is a two-step top coat crackle. This means you apply a medium thick layer of the medium on top of your completed project/surface/or section of a design. When the first step dries, you apply a medium thick layer of the second medium on top. The two layers work to create a crazing on the surface. To see the cracks, you'll then need to apply a darker or lighter color than the background color into the cracks (see project instructions).

SUPPLIES LIST

Delta Ceramcoat Acrylic Paint:
Antique Gold
Antique Rose
Antique White
Barn Red
Black Cherry
Blue Velvet
Blue Wisp
Butter Yellow
Calypso Orange
Candy Bar Brown
Chamomile
Cinnamon
Cornsilk Yellow
Cricket
Crimson
Dark Chocolate
Eggshell White
Gamal Green
Latte
Leaf Green
Lemon Grass
Liberty Blue
Lilac
Lime Sorbet
Midnight Blue
Moroccan Red
Moss Green
Mulberry
Napthol Crimson
Opaque Yellow
Persimmon
Poppy Orange
Purple
Red Iron Oxide
Roman Stucco
Rose Cloud
Sea Grass
Spice Tan
Tangerine
Timberline Green
Toffee Brown
Tomato Spice
Wedgwood Blue
White
Yellow

GLEAMS
Metallic Red Copper

MEDIUMS
Delta products:
Faux Finish Glaze Base-clear
Crackle medium
Fine Crackle Finish Steps 1 and 2
Texture Magic Dimensional Paint—Sienna

MISC. SUPPLIES
Delta products:
Renaissance Foil-Copper
Renaissance Foil-Adhesive
One Step Background Stencil-stars
Whimsical Dot Alphabet-small
Harlequin One-Step Background Stencil
Shadow Alphabet Stencil-large
Circle Foam Stamp
Rubber Stampede "Memories" stamp
Rubber Stampede Girls Play-3732F rubber stamp
Repositionable

Stencil Adhesive
Foam paint roller
Kitchen sponge
1" low tack painters tape
1/4" painters tape
Plastic wrap
Contact Brand Clear Adhesive Shelf Paper
Sea sponge
Palette knife
Cotton swabs
Utility knife
1/2" checkerboard stencil
80 grit sandpaper
Wood filler
X-Acto knife

BRUSHES

Here's a list of brushes I used for these projects. I don't have strict rules for brush use. Whatever works for you, use it! There are, however, a few that are essential to create my style of painting. The others I'll list under recommended brushes. Keep in mind that I'm not foolin' about the essential brushes. You won't get the same effect from a soft hair mop as you will from the mop brush I use. As for the recommended brushes – I'm happy to give you some leeway! If I used a No. 4 round brush, it's recommended you use a round brush, but it doesn't have to be a No. 4. If you only have a No. 2 or No. 6, use one of those brushes.

ESSENTIAL

For this book, I used Loew-Cornell brushes.   For mopping and some of the large-area drybrushing, I used the Series 4, Number 4 duster/stippler. This brush is CHEAP! It comes in a few different sizes (I usually use Number 4) and you can never have enough of them. The brush has stiff bristles which don't absorb as much moisture as regular mop brushes. See the General Instructions for use of this brush. And buy a bunch! If you get a duster/stippler wet, you can't use it again (probably for at least another day). It's handy to have more than

one duster/stippler clean and dry and ready to use. If you want to see what the brushes look like, you can check my website at www.bobpennycook.com. Look under Seminars for the painting seminar project pdf brochure.

To mop smaller spaces, I used the Maxine's mop, Series 270 1/4" and 1/2".

To handle the smaller-area drybrushing and for scumbling color, I used the Series 2014 Round Scumbler in a variety of different sizes, from size 2 to 10. I also used these brushes for the stenciling on these projects.

RECOMMENDED

Loew-Cornell Comfort Brushes
Series 3300 Shader No. 2, 6 and 12
Series 3550 Glaze/Wash 1"
Series 3000 Round No. 2 and 8
Series 3050 Script Liner No. 1

SURFACE SOURCE

All surfaces used in this book are available from Viking Woodcrafts. www.vikingwoodcrafts.com, ph 800/328-0116, fax 507-835-3895

TREE OF LIFE

A simple, whimsical design with lots of texture.
You'll work on your stenciling, stamping and painting skills.

PALETTE

Delta Ceramcoat Acrylic Colors
Gamal Green
Latte
Leaf Green
Lemon Grass
Red Iron Oxide
Roman Stucco
Tomato Spice

SUPPLIES

Oval Cheesebox 25-025M

Delta products:
  Faux Finish Glaze Base-clear
  Texture Magic Dimensional
  Paint–Sienna
  Whimsical Dot Alphabet
  stencil-small
  Rubber Stampede Girls Play-
  3732F rubber stamp
  Repositionable Stencil Adhesive

Palette knife

Utility knife

INSTRUCTIONS

1. Basecoat the top of the lid with Lemon Grass. Basecoat the lid rim with Roman Stucco. Basecoat the bottom of the box with Latte.

2. Mix 4:1 glaze base plus Roman Stucco. Dip the bristle tips of the duster/stippler brush into the mix and wipe off on a paper towel. Drybrush onto the lid, using very little pressure. You want streaky texture to show. Dry well.

3. Mix 4:1 glaze base plus Red Iron Oxide. Use the duster/stippler as in the previous paragraph and drybrush the entire box, including the lid. Dry well.

4. Spray stencil with adhesive following manufacturer's directions. Position stencil at the bottom of the box. Start the stencil with the letter "A" at the box joint then bend the stencil around the box. Using a palette knife spread a thin layer of Texture Magic over the letters. Work all the way around the box, completing the upper case alphabet. Repeat letters as needed. Clean up any overruns with a toothpick, cotton swab or wet paint brush. Let dry overnight.

5. When dry, lightly drybrush the letters with Lemon Grass using the duster/stippler.

6. Using the utility knife, slice the rubber stamp off its wood backing. You need an unmounted stamp in order to bend the stamp around the curves of the box. If you slice carefully, you can always reglue the stamp to the wood block. If you prefer not to slice the stamp, you could try rocking the stamp. Put paint on the stamp (see next paragraph), position the left side of the stamp on the surface and rock the stamp towards the right edge of the stamp using even pressure as you rock.

7. Dip a water-dampened piece of kitchen sponge into Red Iron Oxide. Tap on the entire stamp and press onto the surface. Start at the box joint and repeat the steps all the way around the box. You're looking for texture, not perfection, in the stamping. It's better to have a lighter touch when applying the paint than to put too much paint on the stamp.

8. Mark and tape off a 1/2" band on the lid rim. Stipple with Lemon Grass. Remove the tape. Using a #2 brush, pull short checks of Red Iron Oxide alternating with Leaf Green. Make these random.

9. Transfer the design to the lid.

10. Using a dry, flat brush, pull Lemon Grass Green from the top horizon line down to create the grass. Use very little paint on your brush – you want some texture. Repeat with a little Leaf Green followed by some Gamal Green at the bottom of the grassy area.

11. Tree trunk - use a dry, round brush and loosely base it with Red Iron Oxide. Add touches of Gamal Green to the left and Lemon Grass to the right, while the red it still wet.

12. Brush mix a little Gamal plus Red Iron Oxide and paint short vertical strokes to the left of the base of the tree for shade.

13. Foliage – using the chisel edge of a large, flat dry brush, paint the foliage with Gamal; repeat with Leaf Green and repeat with a little Lemon Grass to highlight. Start in the center of the foliage ball and sweep the color towards the outside edges, lifting the brush as you sweep to create soft outside edges. Add dots of Tomato Spice here and there in the foliage for apples.

14. Paint the swing and ropes with Red Iron Oxide and add touches of Lemon Grass here and there to highlight.

15. Lettering – use a compass or similar marking tool and draw a pencil line about 1/2" in from the bottom of the lid. Place the bottom of the letters on this line and stipple each letter with Red Iron Oxide. The mid point is between the "o" and the "f" of the word "of". Start the stenciling with the "f" and work towards the right "eyeballing" the position of each letter. The work from the "o" towards the left.

Tree

Base and
1st grass color

Leaf Green, shade
on trunk and
2nd grass color

Lemon Grass, trunk
highlight and
3rd grass color

Apples and shade to
bottom left of trunk

MEMORIES BOX

Lifted color creates a subtle texture to the background of this box. Enlarge or reduce the pattern to fit any size box that will best hold your "memories".

INSTRUCTIONS

1. Basecoat the box and top of the lid with Roman Stucco.

2. Mix 4:1 glaze base clear plus Poppy Orange. Brush it onto the top of the lid. Pounce with a soft, slightly damp, kitchen sponge. The objective is to remove color, but you will see some of the base color showing through. Rinse sponge as needed and keep pouncing until you're satisfied with the glaze color. The glaze should appear as a soft orange.

3. Repeat the process on the bottom of the box. Dry well.

4. Basecoat the rim with Red Iron Oxide.

5. Coat the Memories rubber stamp with Roman Stucco and press into place. To paint the stamp, dip a small piece of soft sponge into the paint and lightly tap it onto the stamp. You don't want too much paint. Position the stamp, press the left side of the stamp into place then rock the stamp towards the right edge of the stamp. Apply even pressure to the stamp as you rock it. The wood handle makes the stamp less flexible and to ensure that all the letters are stamped/printed, you need to rock the stamp. Repeat the stamping around the lid rim.

6. Mark and tape off a 1/2" band about 1" up from the bottom of the box. Stipple the band with Red Iron Oxide. Remove tape then dry the paint.

7. Transfer the design.

8. Lid: Using a large round brush with Gamal Green, pull shape-following strokes to paint the petals. Start at the tip of each petal and pull towards the base. The objective is to have good coverage of paint, but with some transparent areas and some ridges to create interest. Dry. Using same brush, mix a little Gamal Green with Antique Gold and pull a few soft-edged highlights on each petal. Dry. Drybrush the petals here and there with Tomato Spice.

9. Brush glaze base over entire top of the lid. Paint Red Iron Oxide around the outside edge and immediately pounce with the duster/stippler to soften and blend the color.

PALETTE
Delta Ceramcoat Acrylic Colors
Antique Gold
Cornsilk Yellow
Gamal Green
Poppy Orange
Purple
Roman Stucco
Red Iron Oxide
Tomato Spice

SUPPLIES
Mini Cheesebox 25-028L

Delta products:
    Faux Finish Glaze Base-clear
    Rubber Stampede "Memories" stamp

Soft kitchen sponge

10. Pears: Base each pear with Antique Gold. Working one pear at a time, brush a coat of glaze base over the entire pear. Immediately dab on Tomato Spice and pounce with the duster/stippler or a small mop to soften the color. You want soft edges to the red but "chunky" color in the middle of the red section. The red should be applied to the left half of each pear. Dry well.

11. Again, brush each pear with glaze base and shade the left and bottoms with Gamal Green, covering the left half of the pear. Dry. Apply glaze base again and shade once more on the left with Purple. Cover only about one-third of the green shade. Dry.

12. Scumble highlights of Antique Gold, followed by Antique Gold plus Cornsilk Yellow, then Cornsilk Yellow, covering a smaller area with each color.

13. Paint the stems with brush-mixed Gamal Green plus Tomato Spice

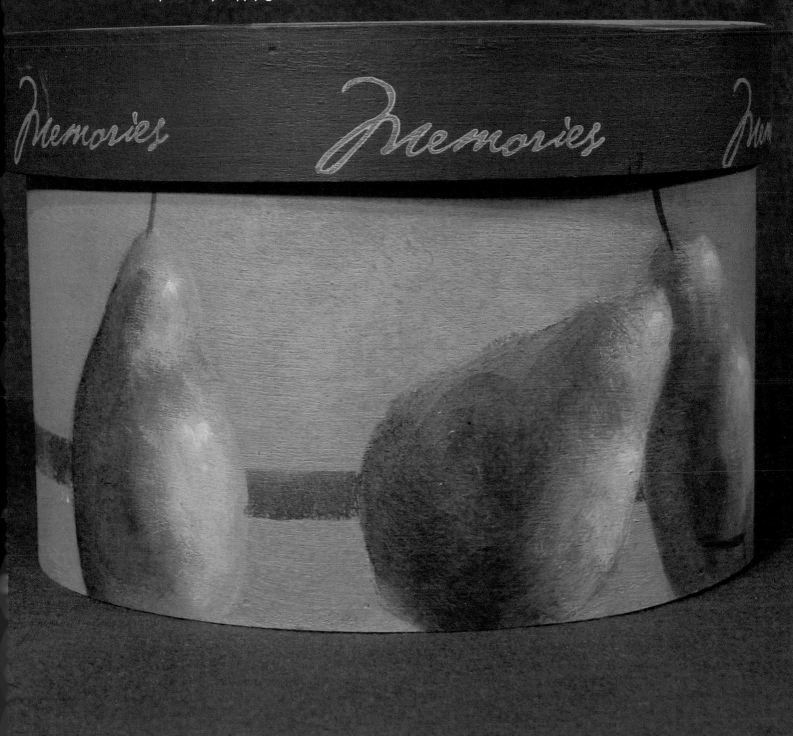

Memories Box
page 8

Easter Basket
page 23

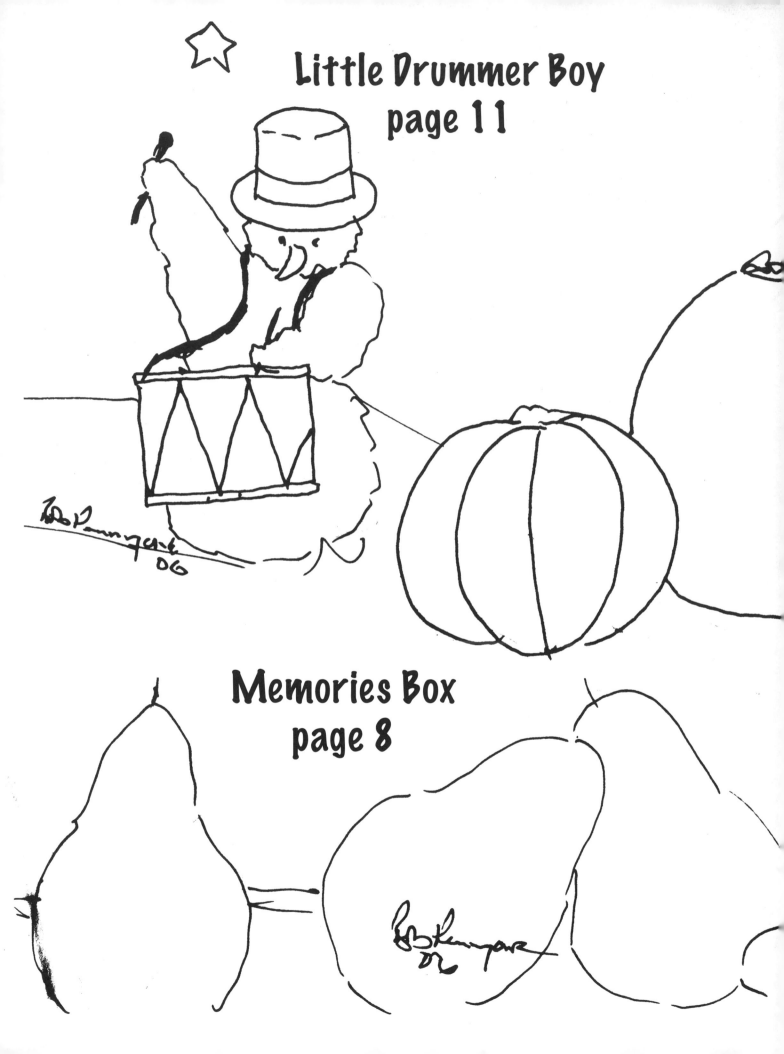

Little Drummer Boy
page 11

Memories Box
page 8

Gourd Oval Box
page 20

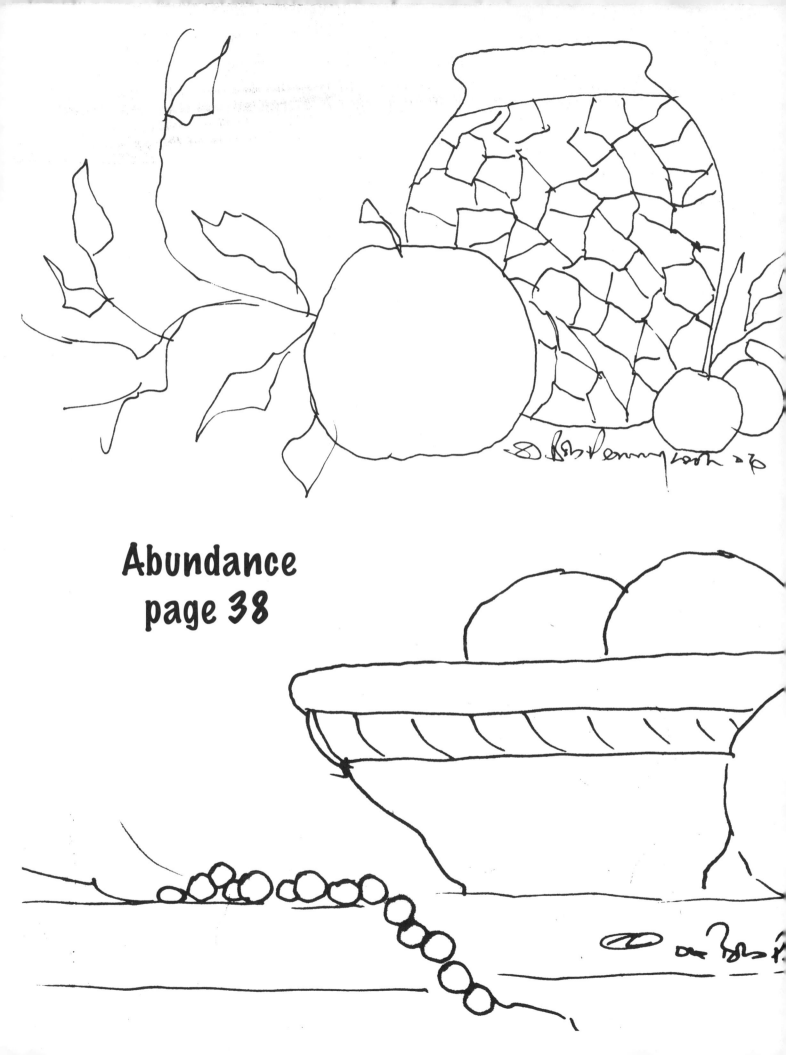

Abundance
page 38

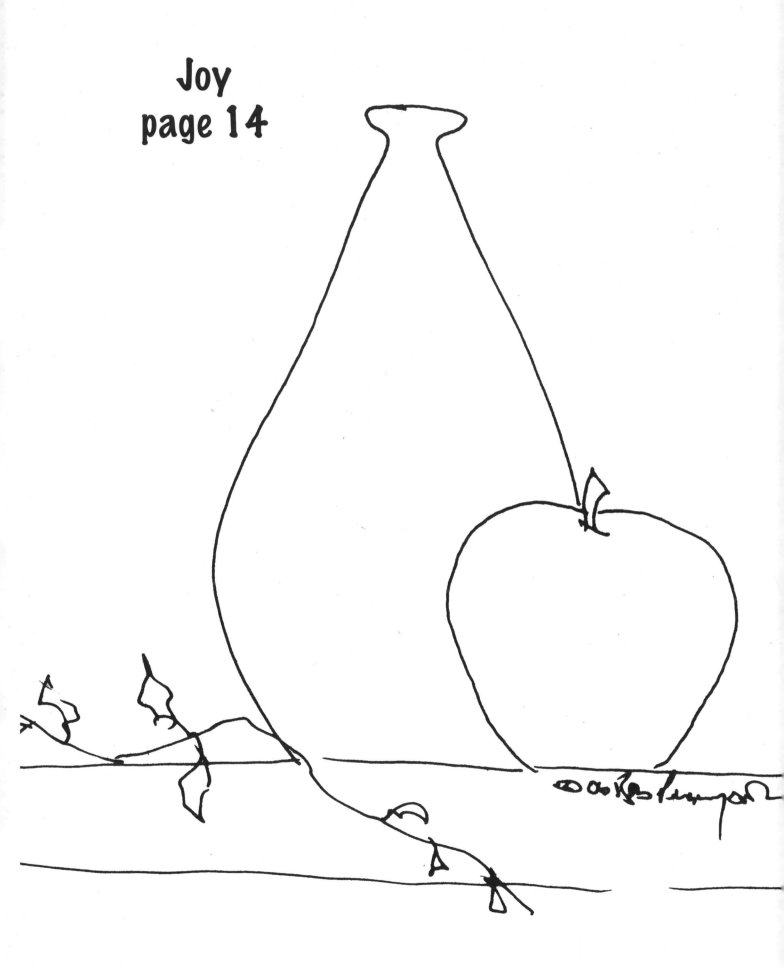

Joy
page 14

8. Re-establish design lines, lightly if necessary.

9. Right and center back gourds: Use a round brush with Gamal Green and roughly stipple the green lines. Follow the traced lines on the design to apply the green. Keep the green narrow at the top and bottom and wider in the middle. Don't try for perfection – it's a roughly colored line. Dab a few spots of Antique Gold here and there on the green. Mix equal parts of Gamal Green plus glaze base. Dip a crumpled piece of plastic wrap into the mix and gently tap onto the gourd. Don't overdo it. When dry, scumble highlights using Cornsilk Yellow, on the upper right of each of the gourd sections. Don't highlight the green sections. When dry, roughly float some Purple down the center of each green line to shade. Float the color here and there rather than creating a perfect floated line. Color should fade towards the right. When dry, brush glaze medium over the left half of each gourd and immediately paint the left side with brush mixed Purple plus Gamal Green. Pounce with the duster/ stippler to soften and blend the color to create shade. The shade should cover almost half the gourd.

10. Green gourd on the left: Use a round brush and roughly dab the tracing lines with brush mixed Gamal Green plus a little Chamomile. Add a little glaze base to the green/chamomile mix and, using a crumpled piece of plastic wrap, dab the mix onto the gourd. Dry well. Brush mix glaze base with a little Gamal Green plus Antique Gold and glaze the entire gourd with this mix. You're aiming for a slight green/yellow cast to the lines and dabs you just added to the gourd. Dry well, and then scumble Cornsilk Yellow on the upper right to highlight. Brush glaze medium over the gourd and shade the left half with brush mixed Purple plus Gamal Green. Pounce with the duster/stippler to soften and blend. Using a round brush with brush mixed Gamal Green plus Purple plus a little Chamomile, dab in the blossom of the gourd at the top. Dab a little Purple plus Gamal Green at the bottom and left side to shade.

11. Remaining two gourds: scumble highlights in the upper right using Cornsilk Yellow. Treat the highlights on the large center gourd as you would a pear- there's a small highlight at the top and a larger highlight on the larger, bottom section of the gourd. Mix equal parts of glaze base plus Gamal Green plus Purple plus Chamomile and dab onto the gourds with a crumpled piece of plastic wrap. Dry well. Load a large brush with glaze base plus a little Antique Gold and glaze each gourd to create a yellow cast. Keep the glaze color out of the highlights. When dry, brush each gourd with glaze base and shade with brush mixed Purple plus Gamal Green. Dab in the blossom at the top of the gourd on the left using the same colors/ steps found in step 10 for the blossom.

12. Stems on the center and right gourds: Base with Chamomile. Using a dry round brush, drybrush the stems with brush mixed Purple plus Gamal Green plus Chamomile. Wipe

the brush and repeat on the left sides and overlaps with Purple plus Gamal Green.

13. Brush glaze base over bottom of the design area. Immediately apply brush mixed Gamal Green plus Purple over the bottom edges of the gourds and on the background. Pounce with the duster/stippler to soften and blend the color. Repeat as necessary, keeping the darkest cast shadow areas to the left of the gourds. On the second gourd from the left, add some of this dark glaze on the bottom and right side of the gourd, where a cast shadow would be created by the front gourd. Dry well.

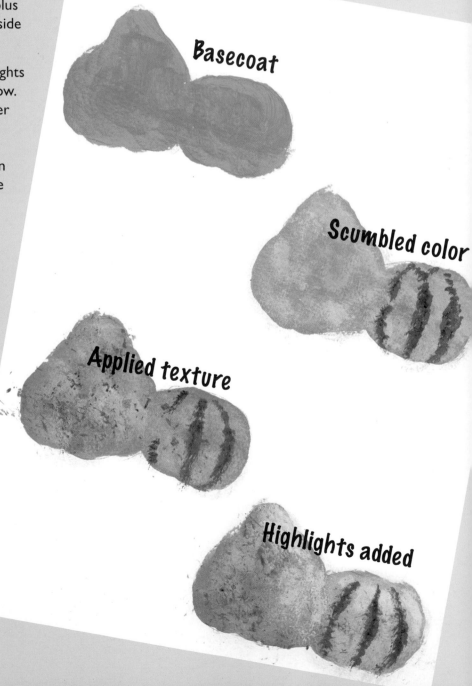

Basecoat

Scumbled color

Applied texture

Highlights added

EASTER BASKET

*A textured background and loosely painted design
make quick work of this whimsical design. The surface is
actually a purse. I chose to leave off the top and make
it a basket — the choice is yours.*

PALETTE

Delta Ceramcoat Acrylic Colors
Antique Rose
Antique White
Liberty Blue
Moss Green
Purple
Rose Cloud
Spice Tan
Toffee Brown
White

SUPPLIES

Colony Purse Box 25-020S

Delta products:
    Texture Magic Dimensional
    Paint–White
    Faux Finish Glaze Base-clear

80 grit sandpaper

Palette knife

Checkerboard stencil (optional)

Wood filler

Sponge — sea sponge, makeup
    sponge or kitchen sponge

INSTRUCTIONS

1. Fill in the vertical grooves in the basket using wood filler.

2. Using the palette knife spread Texture Magic over the entire outside surface below the upper rim. Let dry overnight. Sand with 80 grit sandpaper to smooth out some of the bumps.

3. Basecoat the textured area with Moss Green. Load a large, flat brush with glaze base and a touch of Liberty Blue. Brush over the Moss Green, one section at a time, and wipe back with a paper towel. Lightly sand background to expose some of the Texture Magic.

4. Base the upper rim of the basket and the inside of the basket with Liberty Blue. Drybrush, using the duster/stippler with Moss Green.

5. Base the handle with Moss Green, and using the clean, dry, duster/ stippler, drybrush it with Rose Cloud. Spatter the handle with Liberty Blue.

6. Tape off a 1 1/2" band about 1" up from the bottom. Sponge the band with Antique Rose. Repeat with a light coat of Rose Cloud.

7. Using the stencil (or the #12 flat to pull squares) stipple a checkerboard pattern on the pink band using brush mixed Spice Tan plus Antique White. Roughly paint a double line of Purple at the top and bottom of the band.

8. Transfer the design.

9. Rabbit's basket: Base with brush mixed Purple plus Toffee Brown. Softly mark on vertical lines. Drybrush horizontal bands across the vertical lines from top to bottom using Spice Tan then repeat with Antique White. The center of the horizontal band should be placed over the vertical, traced line. Drybrush Spice Tan then Antique White at the top of the basket to create a rim.

10. With glaze base and a touch of Purple in your brush, create a series of back to back floats down the edges of each drybrushed row and under the rim. Allow to dry. Load your flat brush with glaze medium and a touch of Purple and brush over the left half of the basket and onto the background to the left of the basket. Dry well.

11. Rabbit: Base the rabbit with Toffee Brown and drybrush with Spice Tan. Using the dirty brush, repeat with Antique White, and then add touches of white to highlight the raised areas on the right of the rabbit. Float (using glaze base and a touch of Purple in your brush) the left side of the rabbit.

12. Paint the eyes, nose and mouth using brush mixed Purple plus Liberty Blue. Shade the left sides of each with floats of Purple. Shade the left side, outside of the eyes and nose with Purple, so the color fades to the left. Add touches of Antique White to highlight the nose and eyes.

13. Scrub a little Antique Rose here and there in the ears.

14. The shirt is brush mixed Purple plus Antique Rose, drybrushed with a little Moss Green to highlight.

15. Eggs - Basecoat the egg in the rabbit's hand with Antique White. All other eggs are basecoated with various mixes of Purple plus White or Antique Rose plus White. Line and dot all eggs with various mixes from the color palette. Shade the left side of each egg with a float of Purple. Drybrush a little White on the upper right of each egg to highlight.

25

DAFFODIL BOX

This piece is all about texture; from the loosely painted flowers to the crackled sides.

PALETTE

Delta Ceramcoat Acrylic Colors
Butter Yellow
Candy Bar Brown
Chamomile
Cornsilk Yellow
Eggshell White
Gamal Green
Mulberry

SUPPLIES

Oval Cheesebox 25-024L

Delta products:
    Faux Finish Glaze Base-clear
    Fine Crackle Finish Steps 1 and 2
    Circle Foam Stamp

Kitchen sponge

1" low tack painters tape

INSTRUCTIONS

1. Basecoat the entire box with Chamomile.

2. Using a piece of kitchen sponge, tap Butter Yellow onto the foam stamp and randomly stamp around the entire bottom of the box. This simply creates visual texture and a random pattern.

3. Following the manufacturer's instructions, apply step 1 of the Fine Crackle Finish to the base of the box. When step 1 is dry, apply step 2. Apply both steps relatively thickly. It will take about 15 to 20 minutes for each step of the crackle finish to dry. You need to be in attendance while the medium is drying. Since the medium has been applied to a vertical surface, it will tend to drip. When it starts to form drips, turn the box upside down and let the drips flow in the opposite direction. Repeat until the medium dries. Once the crackle medium has dried, set the bottom of the box aside overnight. This will cure the crackle medium and it tends to strengthen the cracks.

4. The next day, load a large flat brush with glaze base, dip it into Candy Bar Brown and brush it onto the crackled surface. The objective is to get the brown paint into the cracks. Work only a 2 or 3" area at a time, and then immediately wipe it back with a paper towel to remove color from the surface – remember you really only want the brown paint in the cracks to emphasize the cracks. If the glaze base dries before you've removed enough brown paint, dampen the paper towel with water and wipe the color off the surface.

5. After the paint has dried, apply vertical strips of the painters tape around the box and remove every second strip. Using a piece of sponge, wipe Chamomile on the exposed areas. Remove tape and dry.

6. Tape off a band of about 1/2" at the bottom of the box. Use another piece of sponge and wipe the exposed band with Gamal Green. Using the dirty sponge, repeat with Butter Yellow then Cornsilk Yellow.

7. Paint wiggly Gamal Green lines down the edges of the vertical Chamomile bands.

8. Lid: Transfer the pattern.

9. Using the largest round brush you have, paint the leaves and stems with water-thinned Gamal Green. Leave puddles and streaks in the paint to give the foliage some character. Nothing else is done to the leaves or stems.

10. Base the flowers with Butter Yellow. Make sure you can faintly see some of the graphite lines. This will help for subsequent color placement.

11. Using a dry, round brush, drybrush the right edges of the petals and trumpets and the inside areas of the trumpets using brush-mixed Butter Yellow plus Cornsilk Yellow. Repeat with Cornsilk Yellow. Then Cornsilk Yellow plus Eggshell White, followed by Eggshell White.

12. Faintly float Mulberry down the left side of the trumpets, at the base of the opening of the trumpets and here and there on the petals to separate the petals.

13. Repeat the shade here and there with Gamal Green and use Gamal to float under the curl at the top of the trumpet.

14. Add touches of Eggshell White to strengthen the highlight, particularly at the top of the trumpet.

15. Finishing the lid: Apply glaze base over the entire lid.

16. Brush Candy Bar Brown around the outside edge, and then pounce with the duster/stippler to soften the color. Apply color in a strip of about 2 or 3 inches then pounce. Don't try to paint all the way around the lid before pouncing – the color will dry and set before you have a chance to pounce it soft.

17. When dry, repeat the above step, this time using Gamal Green and paint a narrower strip of color around the outside edge.

18. Use a piece of sponge and paint the rim Gamal Green. Using the dirty sponge, repeat lightly with Butter Yellow (you're looking for a drybrush appearance to the paint), and then repeat with Cornsilk Yellow.

19. Add dots of Chamomile around the bottom of the rim.

Base

1st highlight

2nd highlight and
Mulberry shade

Final shading

CHERRY BASKET

Designed with cheery late spring colors and glittering copper accents, this is a quick and easy project to paint.

INSTRUCTIONS

1. Base the basket with Cricket inside and out, except for the inside bottom. Base the inside bottom with Black Cherry.

2. Carefully drybrush the exterior sides vertically with Chamomile then repeat with Eggshell White. Drybrush the interior sides with Black Cherry (lightly) then repeat with Chamomile, followed by Roman Stucco.

3. Base the top band and the handle with Roman Stucco. Drybrush the edges of the handle with Black Cherry.

4. Mark off a 1/2" band at the bottom of the basket and a 1/4" band at the top of the basket and base these with Black Cherry.

5. Transfer the pattern. The supplied pattern shows one double cherry grouping and a single cherry. Place the cherry patterns randomly along the top edge of the Black Cherry band.

6. Cherries: Base with Black Cherry. Drybrush the right half with: Butter Yellow, then repeat, using the dirty brush and covering a slightly smaller area, with Cricket, then repeat with Eggshell White. The drybrush is the highlight side of the cherries. It's better to make the color more intense so it will "read" beneath the red. Wash each entire cherry with Napthol Crimson and add a shine dot in the upper right with Chamomile. Paint the stems with Gamal Green.

7. Paint the word "Cherries" in the center of each panel using Black Cherry. Freehand the letters or print out letters from your computer.

Cherries

PALETTE

Delta Ceramcoat Acrylic Colors
Black Cherry
Butter Yellow
Chamomile
Cricket
Eggshell White
Gamal Green
Napthol Crimson
Roman Stucco

SUPPLIES

Octagon Basket 25-055A

Delta products:
  Renaissance Foil Copper
  Renaissance Foil Adhesive

8. Randomly apply Renaissance Foil Adhesive to the Black Cherry bands at the top and bottom. When dry, apply the foil. What I was looking for here was broken color. Sort of a worn copper look to the bands. The copper shines here and there on the bands, while the base color shows through significantly. It might be good to apply the adhesive with a bristle brush to get even more texture. Don't follow the manufacturer's directions for the adhesive. What you need to do, instead, is apply only one coat of the adhesive; apply it randomly yet apply it smoothly so that all the adhesive dries at the same rate. When the adhesive turns to tacky, apply the foil. Cut small pieces of the foil; lay the foil on the surface shiny side up, and brush vigorously using your fingers only.

Base

Tangerine

Butter Yellow

Cornsilk Yellow

Wash with Crimson

Shade with Gamal

Added highlights